REVITALIZING
Your Board of Directors

■ ■ ■ ■ ■ ■ ■ ■ ■ ■ ■ ■ ■

A Q. & A. Guide
to Getting the Most
from Your
Nonprofit Board

Also by James M. Hardy

Focus on the Family

Using Sensitivity Training and the Laboratory Method (with R.L. Batchelder)

Corporate Planning for Nonprofit Organizations

Managing Individual Development

Managing for Impact in Nonprofit Organizations

Developing Dynamic Boards

REVITALIZING
Your Board of Directors

· · · · · · · · · · · · · · · · · · · ·

A Q. & A. Guide
to Getting the Most
from Your
Nonprofit Board

James M. Hardy Ph. D.

Emerson
& Church
PUBLISHERS

First printed August 1996

10 9 8 7 6 5 4 3 2 1

Printed in the United States of America

Library of Congress Catalog
Card Number: 96-67925

ISBN 1-889102-11-3

This text is printed on acid-free paper.

Copies of this book are available from the publisher at
discount when purchased in quantity for boards of directors
or staff.

Emerson & Church, Publishers
P.O. Box 336
Medfield, MA 02052
Tel. 508-359-0019

TO BETTYE

My wife, best friend, colleague and lover

"In the heart of the world, she will live forever."

Preface

The purpose of this book is to assist chief executives, board chairs, and board and staff members in revitalizing their boards of directors and making them more effective.

I think the reader will find this book different from most others on board development. One of the differences is quite obvious: it's in a question & answer format. The other major difference is more subtle: the questions are from persons who work with real boards and are encountering all of the frustrations, disappointments, fun, and sheer elation that derives from democracy in action.

Like three of my previous efforts, *Revitalizing Your Board of Directors* is designed to be used, not just read. I suggest you begin by reviewing the Summary of Questions, identifying those topics, questions, or issues that you are facing or anticipate facing with your board, and then proceed directly to the selected question and response.

In most cases I think it would be helpful for the chief executive and the board chair to read and discuss the selected responses. This approach will allow you, jointly, to formulate your action plans and agree on responsibilities. At points you may also want the board development committee to read and discuss appropriate responses and formulate the desired action to be taken.

In writing this book I have drawn liberally on material from two of my previous books, *Developing Dynamic Boards* and *Managing for Impact in Nonprofit Organizations*. I'm grateful to Essex Press for permission to use and reference some material from these books.

Most of all I'm indebted to the thousands of board members, board chairs, and chief executives with whom I have worked over the years. Together we have addressed problems, formulated directions, confronted issues and explored new paths - sometimes succeeding and sometimes failing - but it has always been a learning experience for me.

I'm deeply indebted to all of those with whom I have labored and learned. It would be virtually impossible for me to overstate my admiration for them as caring persons and my respect for their countless contributions to our society.

I also want to express thanks to my editor, Jerry Cianciolo. He has organized the material and, as an English major, has been quite persistent in his efforts to improve my syntax and sentence structure and to clarify my frequently muddled writing. At points he has been very picky but, I must admit, he has also been very helpful.

Finally, I'm indebted to my beloved partner for 43 years - my deceased wife, Bettye, to whom this book is dedicated. Her influence is present on each page and in the minds and hearts of all who were privileged to know and love her.

--James M. Hardy

Table
of Contents

Preface
Summary of Questions

Summary
of Questions

Chapter One • RECRUITING MATTERS

Chapter Two • STAYING EFFECTIVE

Chapter 6 • FUND RAISING

RECRUITING MATTERS

1

RECRUITING MATTERS

■ *Balancing the Eight Vital Factors*

My nominating committee recently asked me, the executive director, to furnish them with a list of what qualities, attributes, and skills to look for in new board members. I must admit, I think wealth is the most important, especially since our agency has always struggled financially. If you were asked to furnish a similar list, what would it include?

Having board members who are wealthy may be important, but certainly it isn't the only factor. It may not even be the most important for you. I suggest you take a more comprehensive view.

There are at least two different ways to identify what may be needed in your board: 1) by looking at personal characteristics you desire, and 2) by assessing members against the factors that should be present in your board for it to function effectively.

Let's look first at the kinds of personal characteristics and qualities each board member should possess. You

1.1 probably have several in mind that are important to you. The ones I think are primary include:

❑ Integrity - the ability to know and press for "what is right."

❑ Enthusiasm about your organization and conviction about its mission.

❑ Interest in people - their problems and potentials.

❑ Demonstrated interest in community service.

❑ Willingness to commit time, energy, and resources.

❑ Ability to command community confidence.

❑ Orientation to the future - always looking ahead.

❑ Ability to assess information and make important decisions.

❑ Courage to state one's views on important issues.

❑ Willingness to accept and support decisions democratically made.

With these in mind, let's turn to the *factors* which should be present in your board for it to function well. My experience - supported by research in the field - indicates there are eight important factors, and I suggest you use them as a basis for assessing each of your board members. In random order, these eight include:

1) *Agency expertise*

The degree to which the board member understands your agency's goals, objectives, and ways of functioning. This factor, which can be developed, is necessary for intelligent participation and effective policy formulation.

2) *Management experience*

The degree to which the board member serves in a top level management position in his or her own organization. This factor is important for achieving goals and objectives and to effect changes to keep your agency functioning efficiently.

3) *Community involvement*

The quality, number, and diversity of the board member's other community interests and involvements. This factor is beneficial in meeting community needs and effecting collaboration with other agencies.

4) *Recognition & image*

The degree to which the board member is well-known and whose participation on the board leads to greater community awareness of your agency. This factor is helpful in developing a favorable community image.

5) *Financial impact*

The board member's influence in generating financial support for your agency. Personal wealth makes a sizable contribution possible, but even more important it provides a basis for influencing other support.

6) *Agency commitment*

The degree of involvement (leadership, financial support, participation) of the board member and his or her family in your agency's programs, activities, or circumstances. This factor means the board member has a personal stake.

7) *Community representation*

The degree to which the board and its members accurately depict the interests and needs of relevant groups or classes of people in the community. This factor is beneficial in obtaining input from relevant community groups.

8) *Specific agency service*

The degree to which the board member provides extra or specialized agency services and contacts helpful to your agency's well being. This includes such things as donation

1.1 of skilled time, special legal or accounting services, preferential purchasing status, and funding contacts with corporations, foundations, or public sources.

The relative importance of these eight factors will vary depending on your organization's current status and your goals, objectives, and strategies for the future.

I suggest a group of three persons (yourself, the chair of your nominating committee, and your board chair) determine the importance of each factor for your organization and then conduct an assessment of each board member in relation to the factors (see Q 1.3 for more details on such an assessment).

This procedure will prove helpful in many ways, but especially in identifying the factors you need when selecting and recruiting new board members.

Of course, what I've suggested here involves much more than making a list of desirable qualities, attributes, and skills. It demands an investment of time and energy, but it will pay off for you and your agency now and in the future.

1.2 ## ■ *Personality Types to Avoid*

This is sort of a back-door question. I know the qualities to look for in prospective trustees, let's say integrity, an open mind, and particular expertise, but I want your advice on what personality types to avoid. Are there some types you've encountered who are just too disruptive to bother with?

By all means, yes. Unless you have much more patience than I, you probably want to avoid the following types:

• *Resume Ruth*

The resume builder who wants to be on your board for visibility and a boost in upward mobility in her career, community, or social circle.

• *Commandant Carl*

The authority figure who wants to command, is uncomfortable with group decisions, and is seldom if ever a team player.

• *Single Agenda Annie*

The person obsessed with a single issue and almost completely close-minded to options or differing possibilities.

• *Ego Eddie*

A self-centered soul who raises issues to give speeches or to gain "air time." He has an opinion on everything but seldom has done his homework.

• *Inflexible Ida*

This individual engages in "flight or fight" behavior. She doesn't roll with the punches and is either completely immobilized or overreacts to frustration, conflict, and disruption.

• *Serious Sam*

This guy takes himself and life too seriously. He has virtually no sense of humor and a total lack of enthusiasm.

Finally, I try to avoid the person with no discernible values or principles. It's tough to determine, but even the appearance of shady or slick dealings is troublesome for boards and any conflict of interest, actual or perceived, can be damaging to your organization.

1.3 ■ *Wealthy Members Needed*

The "culture" of our board, if you will, is middle to lower-middle class. How would you suggest we go about recruiting more well-to-do members? My board is timid, and anxious about this, but I'm convinced it's necessary for our long-term health.

It's apparent *you* think your organization needs well-to-do board members, but does your board agree? Probably not.

If I'm correct, then you and, say, two key trustees need to assess your current board against eight major factors that contribute to board effectiveness.

This will show what's missing on your board and help get you where you want to be. The assessment will also assist you in identifying persons in your community who have the factors you need.

One of the eight factors is, of course, financial impact. But there are seven others (as outlined in Q 1.1). These are agency expertise, management experience, community involvement, recognition and image, agency commitment, community representation, and specific agency services.

Your assessment will undoubtedly lead you to recruit new members who bring elements not sufficiently present in your board. When doing so, here are some time-tested recruiting tips to keep in mind.

❑ Carefully select recruitment teams for each prospect. Choose a team of two or three persons whom you believe your candidate respects (peer-to-peer or above is the key).

❑ Understand why you're inviting the person to serve, that is, what his or her specific characteristics are.

❑ Arm each team with thorough information about

your organization - its mission, goals, objectives, and programs. **1.3**

In essence, your recruitment strategy - and you should have one for each of your candidates - should meld the individual's interests, talents, background, and desired factors with your organization's mission, goals, objectives, and desired future.

Try your hardest to find some kind of "personal stake." For example, a small drug abuse organization I know recruited the CEO of a Fortune 100 organization to serve on its board. How? It learned the man's son was recently busted for selling drugs.

One final note: never, ever make an approach by telephone or letter - the job is too important. The appointment should be prearranged and conducted on a face-to-face basis. Recruiting in this way takes preparation and time, but the long-term results more than justify the investment.

■ *Seeking Economic Diversity* 1.4

I'm blessed with an affluent, country-club-like board; trustees literally write me out $10,000 checks over lunch. This is marvelous, but I feel a bit guilty about not having a more economically diverse board. I feel it could bring us different perspectives. Should I encourage my board to seek out people unlike themselves, or am I risking too much this way?

My advice to you is: count your blessings for such a sensitive and generous board; get in touch with, and resolve, your own guilt (the money you're getting, after all, is going

25

1.4 for good things); and, go out to lunch more often!

But, of course, your question is too serious for such flippancy, so let me respond in a more appropriate way.

As you probably know, the question of "representation" is fairly controversial. Many fund raisers state unequivocally that representation diminishes the board's ability to provide necessary funding for the organization.

On the other hand, some leaders in human and social service agencies state as emphatically that relevant programs and services cannot be provided by organizations whose boards are exclusive clubs sorely out of touch with social needs.

I submit that neither position is necessarily correct but either could be correct. It depends on where a particular organization is and where it wants to go.

More than any general rule, making this kind of determination through an organizational self-examination is what is required.

When assessing the composition of a board, there are eight major factors to consider (see Q 1.1). These are agency expertise, management experience, community involvement, recognition and image, agency commitment, community representation, specific agency services, and financial impact.

Your nominating or board development committee, to achieve its desired aims, needs to determine the relative importance of each of these, including community representation and financial impact. It may be that when your agency has completed the assessment, it finds it needs a fairly "exclusive" board (i.e., one high in financial impact, recognition, and management expertise) to move the organization forward.

Even so, your board can still be exposed to "different **1.4** perspectives," as you call them. There are several ways to achieve this but the one I've experienced as most helpful is a Program Advisory Council.

These councils tend to be fairly large groups, as large or larger than your board. They're usually composed of representatives from the different groups you serve or desire to serve (based on gender, race, age, ethnic background, economic level, geography, and the like) as well as persons currently involved in your programs.

Program Advisory Councils provide counsel and guidance to officers of the board, members of the program committee and staff, and to the board itself regarding the effectiveness of programs and services and the needs of different constituencies.

Such councils offer a variety of advantages but mostly they provide a way to keep in constant touch with your agency's programs and services - and their effectiveness. Program Advisory Councils, in other words, are a voice for community people and a way for them to influence programs and services affecting their lives.

Regardless of what direction you take, it won't hurt to have a few more lunches while you ruminate.

■ *Overcommitted Candidates* 1.5

We've identified several strong candidates to join our board. Problem is, other organizations have beat us to them. These individuals serve on seven or eight other boards. Can we realistically expect much from these folks since they're spread so thin? And on how many boards can a person sit before

1.5 | **his or her effectiveness wears thin?**

On your first question - Can you expect much from folks who are spread so thin? - probably not, but the individuals concerned may warrant a try.

Sometimes people serving on several boards develop a special interest in one organization and serve it brilliantly. Can you make serving on your board so challenging, timely, and unique that it will command the best from each member?

If so, go for it - but be honest and forthright in sharing your expectations of what will be involved in serving on your board. In your attempt to recruit busy prospects, be mindful *not* to diminish the importance of board membership with such broad statements as, "Our board won't take much of your time." That's a sure loser.

Remember, too, that a board member's multiple trusteeship can sometimes be a real asset, creating links to other organizations that result in inter-agency collaborations and a focus on community priorities.

Regarding your second question - "How many boards can an individual effectively sit on?" - that depends on the individual and the organization. Usually a person who has achieved success in his or her field and has a large staff can devote more time to civic interests than, say, an entrepreneur with a new business and scarce resources.

Similarly, a growing, dynamic organization usually requires comparatively more time, energy, and resources from its board members than does a rather staid and stable organization. But not always.

If you press me for a number, I'd say for most folks it's about three boards at any one time - plus or minus two.

■ *Guarding Against "Turkeys"* 1.6

We've been burned more than once on recruiting trustees. We take nominations from various people including our current board members and advisory committees, but on at least two occasions in the last year the candidates - who everyone spoke highly of - turned out to be, well, turkeys as trustees. Is there any way we can protect ourselves, other than nosing around about their background and having a solid orientation?

Yes, there are some things you can do without infringing on the privacy of prospects. But understand that a solid orientation and continuous training will help people function more productively as trustees but neither will compensate for poor selection.

I think your nominating committee, or as I prefer to call it, board development committee, needs to be clear on what factors are needed in new board members.

I've cited eight major factors in Q 1.1 and an assessment procedure is detailed in my book, *Developing Dynamic Boards*. It's important to use this or some other assessment method to determine as precisely as possible the factors you need in new board members.

When you've determined what is needed, then you can effectively involve others (current board members, advisory committee members) in generating names of individuals who seem best to fit that need. Lacking this determination, and asking others to suggest candidates, forces them to use their own criteria and results in a hodgepodge of prospects and no objective method of prioritizing them.

Your committee, once you've compiled a list of nominations, can then "weed out" the obviously unqualified

29

1.6 nominees and prepare a "Board of Directors Prospect Sheet" on each remaining nominee.

This sheet provides definitive information on the factors most desired in board members and helps the committee to assess and rank each candidate according to how well he or she represents those factors.

At this point the committee will be in a position to develop a cultivation or recruitment strategy for the most desirable candidates.

The approach I've described here is probably more objective, systematic, and takes more time than what you have been doing. Although I can't guarantee it will eliminate all of your turkeys, I can assure you it will significantly reduce the number.

STAYING EFFECTIVE

. . . .

2

STAYING EFFECTIVE

■ *Keeping Board Service Rewarding*

We have spent the last two years rebuilding our board and in my opinion now have a first-rate group. My question is this: How can I help ensure that these members have a rewarding experience? Or, to put it differently, please outline the best strategies I can use to make sure they stick around a long time.

Do everything you and your board chair can possibly do to encourage each member to participate and be involved in the work of the board.

There are reams of data and scores of volumes attesting to the value of involving people so that they feel a sense of ownership. But fewer than 20 percent of today's managers accept the idea, according to researcher Jay Hall. In light of this, it's ironic that additional research by Dan Fenn, Jr. shows that nearly one-half of corporate executives serving on nonprofit boards feel underutilized.

To achieve the result you want, you and your board chair must take the lead in creating opportunities for involvement.

2.1   You can do this first by conducting a comprehensive board orientation which ensures that members know the job, the agency, and what's expected of them. In addition, you can appoint them to committees or short-term task forces which use their resources. You can also use participatory techniques during each board meeting such as the following:

❑ *Board chair as discussion leader*

Encourage interaction among members, limit "air time" of those who dominate, refer questions back to the group, clarify and restate complex points, summarize periodically, avoid making personal comments that may be interpreted negatively, and don't insist on having the last word.

❑ *Shared leadership*

Delegate responsibilities to different board members for specific activities before, during, and following board meetings; rotate presentation responsibilities among members; minimize staff participation at board meetings - limit it to providing technical or pertinent background information.

❑ *The gatekeeping function*

Help all members participate in discussions by asking questions of individuals or by going "around the table" for responses. Gatekeeping can be performed in relatively simple ways, but with a profound result.

❑ *Subgroups*

Divide the board into subgroups for some agenda items, thus giving each member an opportunity for greater participation. The purpose of subgroups is to generate comments, suggestions, ideas, and proposals for consideration of the total board, staff, or committee.

❑ *Brainstorming*   **2.1**
Use this technique during a board meeting when you need to generate a lot of ideas. It equalizes participation, encourages creativity, and adds excitement and variety to meetings. It can be conducted in small groups (five to seven persons) or in the total board on a free-for-all basis.

Undoubtedly you can come up with additional ideas for increasing participation. It requires some thought, but it's well worth the investment. Plus, you'll provide members with a great experience and they'll be around for a long time.

■ *Avoiding Dependence on a Few*   2.2

On our board of 18 people, we have a handful of workhorses. The problem is, I know - and my staff knows - that they'll always come through, so we tend to overwork them, while other board members just sit passively at meetings or don't bother to even show up. I truly think some of our prized people are growing resentful. We certainly don't want them to resign, so what's your best advice for getting board members to share the load equally?

The first and most important step in resolving the situation is to recognize the problem as you do. But it will be helpful if you also accept the fact that board members will probably never share the load equally.

We all have different talents and live in different situations. Therefore we'll undoubtedly contribute in different ways and at different levels of intensity. That's okay. What's not acceptable, however, is that some are doing nothing.

Take a close, hard look at your situation and be sure that your "workhorses" *want* to share the load. After all, they get a lot of kudos for their work and a bit of ego may be involved.

2.2 Encourage them to get others to participate and to distribute the work load.

I also encourage you, your staff, and your board chair to look closely at yourselves. Are you simply taking the easy way out by calling on the same, reliable folks time after time? If so, agree among yourselves to stop this practice and to broaden the base of involvement. You may, in the beginning, have to do some extra training or even "yoking" - pairing the experienced and inexperienced people and making them jointly responsible for particular tasks.

Finally, be sure your board chair is effectively delegating and giving credit where it's due. Without effective delegation, people will become burned out and your organization will deteriorate. Even more importantly, when board members don't share the load, the organization may continue, but it'll limp along without vitality and zest.

2.3 # ■ *When the Board Splinters*

Over the past two years we've had a few shake-ups on our board and have purposely introduced some diversity. As a result, the board has splintered into various factions. Each of these camps tries - sometimes subtly, sometimes not - to pull me in either direction. And, in fact, I find myself drawn to one of the factions. How do I make us whole again? This current situation is just too draining.

I'm sorry that in your case the cause of your board splintering is directly attributable to increased diversity. It doesn't have to be this way and it saddens me when diversity becomes anything other than a strength for achievement and a forum for learning and insight.

I suppose, however, I must accept this isn't always the **2.3** case and, as in your situation, dysfunctional splintering can result.

In my judgment, you need a strong unifying action for the entire board, a powerful intervention to focus the group on an overriding or even lofty set of tasks. Some examples might include:

❑ Clarifying your organization's mission for contemporary times.

❑ Agreeing on the values that underlie your mission and ways these values might be promoted.

❑ Formulating your organization's five-year goals and expected outcomes.

❑ Defining the major objectives of special projects, programs, or events (such as working with at-risk teens, eradicating racism in the community, collaborating with other organizations in meeting major community needs).

I've found that these kinds of interventions will help people get outside of themselves and focus on goals which transcend individual differences. Very often, in fact, a high level of agreement exists among people but it's overlooked because of the intense focus on disagreement.

For example, a few years ago one of my clients was a large hospital in a racially and ethnically diverse urban community. The conflict between community residents and the hospital was intense: community residents accusing the hospital of racism and malpractice at every turn; people picketing the chairman of the board's law office and distributing flyers proclaiming how unfair the hospital was in serving minorities; others picketing the hospital's operation room and blocking access for physicians; and some even sending letters to the hospital containing letter bombs.

2.3

This situation would, I think, meet most people's description of a "conflict-ridden and splintered environment."

The intervention that turned the conflict around was a meeting I suggested for the hospital's key leaders and community residents. It wasn't based on any complex conceptual model or theory of conflict resolution. I simply placed the attendees in heterogeneous table groupings (mixed to the greatest possible extent by race, gender, and position) and conducted a brief exercise to help them get to know one another. I then asked each individual to describe the hospital functioning at its best in the next five years - an eight minute individual task.

Subsequently, each table group made a composite image of this functioning and reported it to the group. Everyone was amazed. The images for all groups were essentially the same. What these combatants wanted was nearly identical. They had never stopped to understand each other, get clear about their desires, and work together to make it happen.

This is an extreme example, but I hope it makes the point and gives you some ideas for overcoming splintering and building cohesiveness and common purpose in your board.

Finally, I hope you won't back away from diversifying your board because of some initial difficulties. The strengths of diversity far outweigh its relatively minor distractions.

■ *Keeping a Board Challenged* 2.4

Tell me the best ways an august board serving an august organization can maintain a) its vitality, b) its flexibility, and c) its creativity. I feel we're beginning to flag on all three counts.

I'm not sure I know the best ways to keep an organization vital, flexible, and creative, but here are four actions I've found to be the keys to continuous renewal:

❑ *Self evaluation of the board*

You don't need an outside expert and it doesn't take a lot of time. In fact, it's far superior in my judgment for the board itself to generate the data, derive conclusions, and design corrective actions.

I suggest a board evaluate itself twice each year: a "quickie" evaluation during the year, and a more comprehensive one at year's end.

Most good board development books contain forms, designs, and suggestions for both of these kinds of evaluations.

❑ *Involvement of board members*

About half of corporate executives serving on nonprofit boards feel underused. From my discussions with board chairs, it's ironic that most view the use of participatory techniques as not being "businesslike." Indeed, many view participation as a waste of valuable time.

This, of course, is in direct contradiction to research which attests to the need for participation and involvement.

Much can be done to ensure your board members are active outside of board meetings - asking them, for example, to serve as members of task forces, committees, and commissions.

But attention must also be given to involvement *during*

2.4 meetings. No longer can important people be brought together simply to hear reports and vote on routine matters. Increasingly, attention must be given to: sharing leadership and responsibilities before, during, and following board meetings; using small (five to seven-person) subgroups to generate suggestions, ideas, or proposals; brainstorming when fresh thinking and creativity are desired; and, most of all, helping all members get into the board's discussions.

❑ *Planning and review*

Board members must be involved in the strategic planning functions of your organization: developing and/or revising your organization's mission; formulating the long-range goals; generating the necessary financial resources for achieving goals; and monitoring progress at least annually and taking corrective actions.

❑ *Unrelenting pursuit of excellence*

Board members and staff must insist on a continuous search, and striving for, excellence in all organizational endeavors. This must be a shared passion, a total dedication of both board and staff.

Certainly board members need to keep their hands out of operations and management and staff must not engage in governance. But both must insist on the highest level of excellence in fulfilling their roles and in working together. The drive for excellence will bind board and staff together and ensure continuous renewal.

■ *Indicators of an Effective Board* 2.5

I've read much about the barriers to board effectiveness but I'm wondering about the other side of the coin. Will you cite for me the major characteristics that make for an effective board?

There are six major characteristics of effective boards that absolutely leap out of my experience. For me, effective boards:

❑ *Focus on direction, policy, and strategy.*

Effective boards don't try to micro-manage the organization, nor do they become involved in day-to-day operations. Rather, they ensure the organization's mission is clear and relevant, that long-range goals are formulated and set by joint efforts of the board and staff, and that the organization has in place both the policies and the strategies needed to achieve its goals and objectives.

❑ *Ensure the fiscal integrity, stability, and growth of the organization.*

This involves approving the annual budget and continuously monitoring revenues and expenditures in accordance with the budget. Furthermore, it means ensuring that the funds and resources needed to achieve the organization's long-range goals and objectives are provided at sufficient levels and in a timely manner.

❑ *Have strong relationships with the chief executive officer.*

I've never known a board to function really effectively without being undergirded by a strong partnership with the CEO. The partnership should be characterized by creative interaction between the parties and a high degree of interdependence.

2.5

❏ *Are composed of people who are committed and have the attributes, abilities, and skills to move the organization toward its goals and objectives.*

No longer can boards be composed of "warm bodies filling slots." The job is too important and the organization's mission too compelling.

❏ *Create an environment of participation that encourages each person to contribute his or her unique talents and abilities based on the organization's needs.*

Effective boards utilize all members' resources and vigorously resist being dominated by individuals or a small group of "inside" persons.

❏ *Engage in regular self-evaluation and assessment as a basis for continuous board development and improvement.*

Effective boards recognize that development and improvement are ongoing - an unending quest for excellence. They recognize, too, that improvement comes from evaluation and assessment that is periodic but does not consume inordinate amounts of time.

2.6 ■ *Why People Join Boards*

While I know their motivations are mixed, from your experience can you cite one reason above others that volunteers give for becoming board members?

From my experience I believe most people become board members primarily because they believe in the mission of an organization and want to be a part of actualizing that mission in the lives of people and in the community being served.

There's a chance I'm fooling myself. The Edmonton Social Planning Council in Edmonton, Alberta, Canada did a study of why people volunteer to serve on boards. It **2.6** identified 13 major reasons and my primary reason was not directly included in their results.

Indeed, over two-thirds, 69 percent, of the reasons given were related to receiving personal benefits (i.e., acquiring special skills, being with others, recognition and status, actively utilizing leisure time, and the like).

I'm certainly not opposed to board members receiving personal benefits - in fact, I think it's vital they receive as well as give. Still, my experience indicates that the vast majority and usually the best board members are motivated by high, noble, and altruistic purposes of human service.

Overly idealistic? Perhaps, but I don't think so.

■ *Board Self-Evaluation* 2.7

Our board is like most, I assume. Some members work like the dickens, some do only what they're asked, other might as well be stones. I'd like to implement some system of evaluation, where the board evaluates itself, hopefully to expose the laggards. What's your opinion of formal board self-evaluation and are there any you can recommend?

Formal board self-evaluations can be very helpful. In fact, I agree with Kurt Lewin who argued that *self*-evaluations, in general, are just as valuable as those done by outside experts or researchers *if* an effective process is used.

There are scores of approaches to evaluating or assessing your current board (and I assume by evaluation you mean assessing each member in relationship to what's needed to make your board effective). To be completely immodest, I

2.7 must say the most useful self-assessment approach I know of is the one described in Chapter 4 of my book, *Developing Dynamic Boards.*

This assessment is conducted by a team of three people - the board chair, executive director, and the chair of the nominating or board development committee. Eight factors are assessed: agency expertise, management experience, community involvement, recognition and image, financial impact, agency commitment, community representation, and specific agency service (see Q 1.1).

These factors are explained and clarified for the organization and a weight is assigned to each. The team's task is then to review each board member and agree on a rating for each factor. By using some fairly simple mathematics, an index is computed on each member's value in relation to the factors and to the organization as a whole. It's like a batting average. The heavy hitters and light hitters (and no-hitters) are clearly identified.

This evaluation provides a basis for deciding which specific actions can be taken to support particular board members in increasing their effectiveness. It also supplies the data for identifying deadwood and developing a strategy for "retiring" them.

Conducting an assessment of this kind is a great way to begin a board development program. I wholeheartedly recommend it. In responding to your question, however, I'm certain I've made the process sound more complex in written form than it actually is in practice. It's almost like Mark Twain said of Wagner's music, "It's not as bad as it sounds."

■ *How Long Should a Board Member Serve?*

Two related questions: What, in your opinion, is the optimum tenure for a trustee, and, do you recommend a (mandatory) period of time off for trustees?

Optimum tenure is a tough question which, for some people, defies generalization. But as difficult as it is, I think we need to generalize a policy for all board members, one that applies equally to everyone.

I prefer two three-year terms of continuous service with one year off before eligibility for reelection. This gives the best board members six continuous years of service. (I needn't remind you that reelection is never automatic for *anyone* - it's reserved solely for board members performing well.)

A year off provides respite for effective board members from the routine of regular board meetings. It also allows for a flow of "new blood" that can be revitalizing and energizing.

If you do rotate outstanding board members off the board, however, be sure they know it's only for a year, and keep them involved through committee appointments, special assignments, and advisory roles. Don't risk losing them forever by ignoring them.

2.9 ■ *Merit to Emeritus?*

Do you find any value in emeritus status?

Yes, there is value in emeritus status for selected board members. It can offer significant recognition to those who have rendered extensive and exemplary service. But emeritus status shouldn't include voting privileges and responsibilities.

While the loyalty and dedication of most emeritus appointees will remain steady, their knowledge of your organization - and the environment in which it's currently functioning - won't be as current as it was during their years of full activity. Voting rights should always be the province of board members who are intimately involved and informed.

2.10 ■ *When Board Members Don't Act Like Owners*

My problem is a subtle, albeit, important one. My board members think of themselves primarily as helpmates to the organization rather than the owners of it. That's useful in the sense that almost all of them roll up their sleeves when, say, there's a fund raising event to organize. But the downside is they don't assume full responsibility for the organization. They tend to view it as a sort of agreeable pastime, implicitly passing the buck back to me as director. How can this state of affairs be changed?

It's good you have board members who are helpmates and will roll up their sleeves and get involved in hands-on service. But, as you imply, that's not enough.

It very well could be that your board members aren't

acting like owners because they perceive *you* to be the | **2.10**
owner. They do things to help you out because they probably believe in what the organization is trying to accomplish.

If this is true, I think that with the support and assistance of the board chair, you need to involve your trustees in work for which they must shoulder responsibility - formulating long-range goals, monitoring progress, developing policies, generating resources, and the like.

I suspect this will be difficult to do, especially at first, because board members have become so dependent on you for these things.

Consider such measures as: a board retreat or an off-site conference for more in-depth work on governance tasks; one-on-one briefings of board leaders on getting involvement in policy issues; and discussions on governance roles.

To develop your board into a strong and effective governance group, work with them. Don't relieve them of the responsibilities of governance and resist the temptation to do their job - something that's hard to do because it's so ego supportive.

■ *Board Rehashes, Doesn't Lead* 2.11

My board, which is pretty high-powered, spends most of its time - I'd say 85 percent - reviewing and rehashing what my staff and I have already done. This seems wasteful to me. What strategy can I use to prompt them to lead rather than review? They're a very talented group.

It's inevitable for a board to spend some time reviewing work done by staff. That's an important part of keeping the

2.11 board informed and knowledgeable about the organization and its work. But I agree that 85 percent is much too much.

If you want the board to lead, you and your board chair must create the opportunities to do so. Your best strategy, I think, is an overnight board retreat.

Pick a real need as your focus, one requiring leadership, such as formulating five-year goals *or* reviewing your mission *or* updating your organization's long-term direction based on last year's performance. There are many such topics that require caring, wisdom, and objectivity - the very characteristics that it sounds like your board possesses.

I also strongly recommend an annual retreat for boards. Typically, you accomplish a lot of work that simply can't be done in monthly meetings. And there are ancillary benefits as well: learning to work together, getting to know each other as persons, understanding the organization and getting in touch with its "soul." All of this in addition to some old fashioned fun, relaxation, and fellowship.

Yeah, I know - you say you can't get them to attend. Do the following three things and I'll guarantee a good attendance: 1) get a core group of key board persons, four or five, to commit to the idea, 2) give everyone plenty of lead time to put it into their schedules, two or three months at least, and 3) ask your key leaders to make individual contacts to encourage attendance.

It will take some time and effort but it's worth the investment.

■ *Remember the Mission*

Our organization has a noble mission, but you'd never know it from attending our board meetings. We're always focusing inward, on details, mechanics, and systems. What I want to know is, how I can "keep the dream alive" in our meetings so that everyone sees the relationship of mundane things like budgets and audits in the context of the noble goals we've come together to achieve? Please help!

I really like your phrase "keep the dream alive." In fact, if I had to capsulize the primary job of the CEO and the board chair, that phrase would do it. But it's not easy to accomplish.

There are all kinds of measures you can take in your regular meetings to keep the organization's "ultimate results" in the board's consciousness. Have some of the recipients of your services meet with the board to share activities and testimonials. Have program staff describe some of the most exciting new developments. Or, have the board visit program sites and observe programs in action. Try to have one such ingredient in most board meetings.

But the most important suggestion I have is this. At the next board meeting, divide the board into subgroups of about five members each and ask them, for a period of 10 minutes, to brainstorm ideas for "keeping the dream alive." You can bet on one thing - what they develop will be better than what I've suggested and even more important, they will "own" the ideas.

2.13 ■ *Class Conflict*

On our 12-member board we have a number of "high status" people. They are the most talkative at meetings and are subtly accorded the most respect. Other members are intimidated and deferential (I can barely pry a word out of some of them). What's the best way to deal with this imbalance?

There are two fairly obvious ways to deal with your problem: one, build the board so it's composed *entirely* of "high status" people; or two, find ways to help the intimidated people participate more *while at the same time* encouraging the status folks to be more sensitive and accepting.

The first option will lead you in the direction of a more homogeneous board — this at a time when I think you really need a variety of characteristics, experience, and talents. Consequently, I suggest you think of specific ways to increase the involvement of the quiet members. Here are some ideas:

❏ *Give them responsibilities*

There are a variety of functions and activities to be performed at board meetings and they shouldn't all be done by the officers. Indeed, responsibilities for specific activities before, during, and following board meetings should be delegated as much as possible to the less talkative members.

Here are some examples:

Before - Ask the quiet people to write a letter to members encouraging attendance and participation at board meetings or special events.

During - Ask quiet members to lead an ice breaker exercise at the beginning of the next meeting or to be a "process observer" and to report observations at the next meeting.

After - Ask quiet members to do follow-up telephoning or visits regarding such matters as assignments, briefings for absentees, or solicitations.

You might also suggest to committee chairs that presentation responsibilities be rotated among members rather than always falling to the same few persons.

❑ *Perform the gatekeeping function*

In terms of involvement techniques, probably none is as significant as that of gatekeeping. Although some theorists might express a contradictory point of view, I think in your case the gatekeeping function should be the responsibility of the board chair and the CEO, rather than hoping all members will be gatekeepers.

When effectively performing the function, the gatekeeper opens up communication channels by encouraging or facilitating the participation of others, or by demonstrating actions that regulate the flow of communication so that everyone has a chance to contribute.

For example, you or the board chairperson might simply ask a silent member a question like, "Jim, you've been in a number of similar situations. What do you think about this matter?" Another way to "open gates" is for the chair to "go around the table" and ask each person to state *briefly* where they are on the issue under discussion. Gatekeeping can be performed in relatively simple ways, but with profound results.

❑ *Divide into subgroups*

For some agenda items, it can be helpful to divide into subgroups — particularly for those items that call for board review and reaction, and for those requiring input, suggestions, and proposals from the total board.

2.13   Subgroups keep members more involved by giving each person an opportunity for more "air time." Such groups should never be charged with making major decisions, however. To be effective, subgroups should be 1) small - about five people, 2) well instructed in terms of tasks, expectations, and guidance, 3) assigned a short work time - such as 15 minutes, and 4) prepared to report using flip charts or other visual aids.

Depending on the success of your efforts to increase involvement, the board chair may also want to meet face to face with the "high status" members. Here the board chair can bid for increased sensitivity to the less talkative members and support for increasing their involvement and participation. If utilized as a part of the solution, the "higher status" members can probably find ways to be helpful in ensuring that all viewpoints are expressed.

2.14   ## ■ *Board Retreats*

How often should we hold a board retreat? I say yearly, but my board balks and says every two years is plenty. What do you say?

There's no magic frequency for board retreats. I think it's helpful to have an annual retreat if there's a compelling board task to be accomplished that can't be done in regular meeting times and if the board is motivated to get away and work on the task.

It's highly desirable to have a two-day retreat to formulate your long range goals. It's also critical to have an update and review of the goals annually. This update and review can usually be accomplished in about four working hours, assuming extensive preparatory work is done. Obviously the board can do this work without getting out of town. **2.14**

There are, of course, ancillary benefits to conducting off-site board retreats: participants get to know each other better in an informal and relaxed atmosphere, and they become more knowledgeable about the organization through informal discussions and fellowship. However, the benefits are more than offset if, due to apathy and lack of interest, attendance is low.

■ *Main Barriers*   2.15
to Board Effectiveness

From your experience, will you please describe what you consider to be the main barriers to board effectiveness?

In my opinion, there are five barriers that can greatly inhibit, if not preclude, effective board functioning:

❑ *Board composed by the wrong criteria.*

This happens when an organization fails to decide systematically which factors are needed in its board composition to achieve its goals. So often organizations take the easy way (i.e. "Who can we get to serve?") rather than select board members because they have attributes, abilities, skills, and experience the organization needs.

❑ *Board trying to manage rather than govern.*

This results in staff being reduced to "gofers" rather than professionals and eventually leads to a dependency and tension that's dysfunctional.

Typically this is done through information control - only letting the board and others know what the executive director

2.15 wants them to know. This makes the board completely dependent on the executive and it too results in dysfunctional relationships and tension.

❑ *Ineffective board and staff relationships.*

This happens when the board and staff are functioning independently rather than interdependently. I've never known a board to function really effectively without being undergirded by a strong partnership with the staff.

❑ *Sporadic and inadequate board development.*

All boards must be continuously developed in order to maintain their effectiveness. This involves ongoing assessment of the board's composition; identification of board members; cultivation; recruiting new members; retiring unproductive members; board orientation and training; use of members' resources; evaluation of board functioning; and recognition. And that's just to name a few components of board development. The board chair and the executive director must, in my judgment, give leadership to this continuous effort.

PROBLEM BOARD MEMBERS

••••••••••

3

PROBLEM
BOARD MEMBERS

■ *Wholesale Board Changes*

3.1

I've just been hired as the CEO for an agency I believe deeply in but for whose board, particularly the chairperson, I have no professional respect. Don't get me wrong. These are five dear people but they simply aren't equipped to address the challenges we face. How do I go about replacing the entire board, most especially the chair? We're strapped for cash, our programs are sagging and I need to move fast!

Go ahead and move now on improving your fiscal management and cash flow position and on increasing the effectiveness of your programs. That, after all, is probably why they hired you and pay you that big salary. Get on with it!

But I suggest you not attempt to change the chairperson and your entire board in the immediate future. That's going to take more time, if it occurs at all.

It very well could be that your board of five people is too small. Assess this yourself and, if you agree, develop a strategy to: identify the kinds of factors that need to be present in your

3.1 board and to what extent; identify the persons in the community who possess these factors; and recruit the desired persons and orient them to your agency and their role, functions, and relationships (see Chapter One). I suggest you involve at least two of your present board members in accomplishing these tasks.

In terms of changing your chair and current board members, make that decision in about a year. You're new in your job and need to work with your board. You've got to struggle, cajole, accomplish, and make mistakes as you work together and, hopefully, move steadily toward forming a productive partnership.

3.2 ## ■ *Do-Little Chairperson*

I've got a committee chair who, in board meetings, talks a wonderful game. To listen to her, you'd think she's the ideal volunteer: articulate, organized, and efficient. But it's all a charade. In between meetings she doesn't give this organization a second thought. We desperately need to relieve her (even though her term is only a few months old). But because she's so skillful at camouflaging her inactivity, the other members can't see it. Please help me with a solution.

Forget relieving her. You've got to make it work for at least a few more months. Get on with your job of establishing a relationship and helping her successfully carry out her responsibilities. Specifically, I suggest that you:

❑ *Meet regularly on a face-to-face basis.*

Hold meetings at least monthly and probably more often at the beginning. It takes time and investment to develop a productive relationship. In these meetings, take time to really get into some issues, catch each other up on developments, and provide mutual counsel and help.

❏ *Be open, candid, and straightforward.*

There should be no organizational secrets between you. Both of you must share the same information for your leadership to be complementary. Some conversations will undoubtedly be private while others may be personal. Both of you must honor these confidences.

❏ *Communicate and communicate some more.*

The need is for continuous and timely communication. Each of you should help the other's involvements to be as surprise-free as possible. Each must be sensitive to the need to return calls quickly and to be available to the other when needed.

In a nutshell, quit whining and get on with your job of developing people's leadership qualities for your organization.

3.2

■ *Self-Serving Service*

3.3

I feel we have a pair of trustees who use their status as board members to enhance their resumes and gain status in the community. They rarely attend board meetings, don't contribute, nor do they have time to raise money. Still, they value their status as board members for their own career goals. How do we move them towards more active status or nudge them out?

Board members should receive benefits from their service and from making valuable contributions to the agency. The fact that these benefits for your two board members involve better resumes, increased status, and a push up their career

3.3 ladder is great. But it's not acceptable if they don't contribute.

Assuming you're the executive director, I suggest you and the board chair discuss this thoroughly, plan your strategy, and have a private, face-to-face meeting with each of these board members. The watchwords for you and your board chair during these meetings are *candor* and *sensitivity*.

In a very forthright way, your board chair must make clear what's expected of each board member and the inadequacy of these individuals' performance. During the entire discussion, you and the board chair must be sensitive to each person's situation and feelings and any extenuating circumstances.

Based on what you've said, it's hard to predict the results of these conversations. On the one hand, it may be that the two people will want to continue as board members and agree to be more responsible in the future. If so, be sure you are specific with regard to expectations and agreements.

On the other hand, they may for whatever reasons not be able to fulfill the responsibilities. In this case, you and the board chair need to make it clear that you must have people on the board who can carry out the necessary duties and be actively involved in moving the agency toward its mission and goals. Express appreciation for their past services and, if it can be done in a genuine way, provide recognition for what they have contributed.

Of course, the outcome of your conversations may fall somewhere in between the two extremes that I've described. If so, you must adapt your actions accordingly.

■ *Business Leaders as Board Members*

A majority of our board members - high powered executives in their everyday life - don't consider our organization a business. As a result they don't apply the same common sense standards to decisions they make on behalf of the organization, many of which are out-and-out dumb. I see their behavior as paternalistic and want to know how I can prevent them from checking their business acumen at the door.

If it's any consolation, the problem you describe isn't a new one. It was identified years ago by Dan Fenn, Jr. in a national study of business executives in their role of policy makers in nonprofit organizations ("Executives as Community Volunteers," Harvard Business Review, 1971).

Fenn concluded, "When the businessman walks into the board room at the Y, or the hospital, or the school, or the community action agency, he apparently leaves his leadership hat outside the door - even in the areas he knows best and likes best." Somewhat ironically, the study also found that nearly half of the corporate executives serving on nonprofit boards feel underutilized.

I think there are a number of actions you can take to use the resources of business persons on your board more fully:

❑ *When recruiting business persons, emphasize your need for their management experience.*

Personally, I avoid saying nonprofits are businesses. I don't want to get immersed here in semantics and I do recognize that nonprofit boards need, as you say, "business acumen," but to me nonprofit organizations are different

3.4 | from business organizations.

Their purpose is social profit not financial profit. Both kinds of organizations, however, do need management experience and expertise. And when you recruit persons from business you need to make this clear from the outset.

❑ *Conduct an interactive orientation program for all new board members.*

Fenn's research indicated that only 15 percent of board members reported having any formal (or informal) training or briefing to prepare them to serve on the organization's board. Compile a board manual for each member and be sure your orientation covers: agency mission, goals, philosophy, and functioning; major functions of the board of directors; responsibilities of individual members; board and staff relationships; board and staff partnership; and board calendar of meetings and activities.

❑ *Put them to work.*

Provide real, meaningful, and important tasks that make use of their resources. These might include formulating your agency's long-range goals and expected outcomes, developing strategies for achieving goals, ensuring that financial resources are available, monitoring achievement of objectives and the resulting impact on goals.

Do these things and you won't find business persons leaving their "business acumen" outside your board room nor will you find them feeling underutilized.

■ *Handling the Devil's Advocate*

On our board we have a fellow who gleefully plays the devil's advocate - at any and every turn. No matter the idea, no matter the consensus, he loves to jump in with his "But on the other hand..." and dominate the floor for 10 minutes. He really slows down our meetings and impedes productivity. What's the best way to deal with such a person?

First off, I suggest asking yourself, "Is this guy really impeding the progress and productivity of the board or is he simply a big pain in the backside for me?"

I've known trustees who were perceived by some to be resistant to change or defenders of the status quo because they were interminably raising questions, making comments, and slowing down the process of decision-making. In many cases, however, these people made significant contributions to the debate.

More specifically, they forced the board to be more analytical, pushed for the examination of alternatives, called into question pet ideas or vested interests, and caused proponents to clarify and provide appropriate rationale.

In short, these interventions were helpful though their constancy made them painful. Every board needs these "loving critics," as John Gardner called them.

However, if your board leadership is convinced that this member's behavior is in fact harmful, then the chair needs to have a face-to-face chat with him.

In this private conversation the chair should be very specific in describing the person's behaviors and their effect on board functioning. My hunch is, this will solve the problem.

3.5

However, if it begins to rear its head again, the chair shouldn't hesitate to deal with it directly, politely, and firmly in board meetings. Dominance of this sort, that inhibits or impedes the board in fulfilling its responsibilities, simply cannot be permitted.

3.6

■ *Retiring Ineffective Trustees*

Describe for me the best scenario for removing an inert trustee from our board.

It seems to me that removing or "retiring" a trustee before the end of a term should be the action of last resort. Prior to that, every effort should be made to activate the person. Here are a couple of ideas to try:

1) Your board chair might have lunch with the person, not only to describe what's expected of board members but also to engage him or her in a discussion of the board's role and the responsibilities of individual members.

2) Get the individual involved no matter how small the assignment. It's possible that even a modest task will spring the person loose and propel him or her back to action. It's also possible the person will conclude that he or she should no longer serve.

If nothing works and it's clear you have deadwood on your hands, then you're right, you must make a move.

All too often, organizations don't replace unproductive board members. Their rationale is one I hear all the time: "We can't replace board members. They're elected." Nonsense. A seat on your board is too important to be filled by a person who isn't contributing.

I suggest your board chair and executive director invite **3.6**
the person to lunch and, in a direct but sensitive way, request
that he or she relinquish the position, explaining that the
current direction of the organization requires different kinds
of resources. Depending on the person and circumstances,
future service in the form of an advisory or honorary position
might be suggested.

In any event, be sure to recognize the individual's service.
I've found that many currently inert trustees have rendered
significant service in the past and have simply run out of gas.
They can and should be provided genuine and meaningful
recognition.

I've also found that even though a direct and forthright
approach is seldom used in dealing with non-performing
trustees, when it's done in a sensitive way it's appreciated.
We're kidding ourselves if we think people don't realize they
aren't contributing. Some may even be feeling guilty about it
and will be greatly relieved.

■ *Do "Letterhead" Trustees*   3.7
Have a Role?

**What's your opinion of "letterhead" trustees? Do
they lend any credibility to an organization even
when they're not asked to do any real work?**

I don't think so-called "letterhead" trustees are helpful to
an organization. In fact, "letterheads" can impair the effective
functioning of a board. It's degrading to other trustees to have
people who never attend or work to carry the title of "trustee."
It belittles the job.

If you have a prestigious person who can't attend meetings

3.7 or work as other trustees do, try using him or her as a public spokesperson for your organization - someone who makes public service announcements and media statements about you. The individual may be challenged by this assignment and possibly lend your organization some credibility.

There are, of course, many other ways to use the resources of letterhead trustees, depending on the nature of those resources. I encourage you to do so, as it can be fulfilling for the individual and provide needed services and credibility for the organization.

Even so, it is important to recognize that providing service and specialized resources is a far cry from fulfilling the organization's ongoing governance responsiblities.

Make use of people's resources, but don't make the mistake of filling a trustee's chair with someone who's not attending and helping your board fulfill its vital governance functions.

3.8 # ■ *Ill-Prepared Chairperson*

My board chair, God love him, likes to "wing it." Even though I regularly send him a preliminary agenda, he ignores it. He feels cocky enough to glance at the agenda a minute before we start. The problem is, our meetings often get off track and little is accomplished. How can I persuade him of the importance of preparation?

It sounds to me like neither of you are doing the kind of agenda preparation necessary for an effective board meeting. Let me explain.

The best procedure I've found for developing agendas is a face-to-face meeting approximately two weeks prior to the board meeting. If yours is a large regional or national organization, then you may have to do it by telephone.

In preparation for this meeting, you (the CEO or executive director) and the board chairperson should make a list of possible items for consideration based on a review of past board minutes, reports or recommendations from committees, emerging issues that require consideration, and information items that must be presented for the board's edification.

At this preliminary meeting, the two of you must decide which of the items will be included on the next board agenda. In general, priority should be given to action items requiring immediate decisions by the board versus those that might be considered at a later meeting.

Once you and the chairperson have agreed upon the specific agenda items, be sure to consider the format and flow of the meeting. Contrary to conventional wisdom, I don't think it's necessary to follow a set order of business for each meeting. Variety in order and method is highly desirable and relieves monotony.

One caution: beware of "loading the agenda" and creating a frustrating situation in which the agenda isn't completed within a specified time frame, or action items are rushed and not given sufficient deliberation time

The kind of agenda preparation I'm describing will result in genuine "ownership" on the part of your board chair. He will adhere very closely to the items and the order in the actual meeting - no more getting off track or winging it. You can bet on it.

3.9 ■ *Inconsistent Attendance*

Here's my dilemma. About nine months ago we recruited a super-wealthy person (he's on the Forbes 400) to join the board. He came to the first meeting, then skipped the next two, then made a perfunctory appearance at the fourth. It's becoming apparent that either he doesn't want to attend our meetings or his schedule is so full he can't. Should we let this go on, content with the potential of his financial support? Or should we take a different tack and, if so, what?

I don't think you should let it go on.

A colleague of mine believes that when a board member misses three successive meetings near the beginning of his or her tenure, then the person is essentially lost to your organization. I agree - it's time to act.

The board chair and possibly the chief executive or the vice chair should take the new member to lunch. With candor and great sensitivity, you need to acknowledge that the person was missed at the board meetings, and be very straightforward in explaining what the agency is trying to do and why attendance is so important.

Be prepared to offer specific suggestions for increasing the individual's involvement (i.e., special assignments, specific responsibility at the forthcoming board meeting). This may rectify the problem or it may elicit an explanation of how the individual's situation has changed since agreeing to serve on the board.

If this change involves a temporary condition that will be resolved in the near future, then it can probably be accepted without further attention. On the other hand, if the change is permanent and will result in highly sporadic board attendance,

then you will probably need to request that the person resign | **3.9**
from the board and accept an assignment on a committee or
task force that will not demand regular meetings.

In my opinion, no one, not even a Forbes 400 listee,
should be on your board without contributing time, talent,
and resources. As authors Lippincott and Aannestad have
pointed out in a *Harvard Business Review* article, attendance
at board meetings is perhaps the greatest indicator of the
health of your agency.

■ *Passive Boards* 3.10

**Why, even though boards are owners of the
organization and have the power to guide and
direct it, are they almost always passive? There must
be some dynamic going on that you can enlighten
me about.**

If there is a single dynamic that causes passivity, it's the
lack of "ownership" on the part of board members. I'm not
talking about legal ownership (which is specified in your
constitution and bylaws), I'm referring to a more emotionally-
based sense of ownership - a genuine feeling that "this is
mine," whether it's a decision or the entire enterprise.

A lot of things can block or at least inhibit board members
from feeling this sense of ownership:

❑ Members are uninformed with respect to their roles
and functions.

❑ Members' talents are not used.

❑ Meetings are dull and unproductive with few
opportunities for real involvement.

❑ The board chair and CEO or a small group decide on

3.10 major policies or plans.

❑ The board is overly involved in day-to-day operations to the detriment of governance functions.

❑ Strong staff dominate all affairs of the agency. And,

❑ There is little or no understanding of the relationship between board and staff and the board/staff partnership.

If we want boards to be active rather than passive, vigorous rather than lethargic, to provide leadership and thrust rather than coast, then we must provide for real, genuine, and meaningful involvement of all members. This, in essence, is the job of the CEO and the board chair.

BOARD & STAFF RELATIONS

. . . .

4

BOARD & STAFF RELATIONS

■ *CEO Possessive about Board*

My boss, the executive director, is very possessive when it comes to working with our board. She wants to be the only person who interfaces with members. So, rather than my going directly to the development committee chair, she insists I explain what I need to her and she'll bring it to the chair. I can understand that, as director, she needs to be kept fully informed but this seems to be an ineffective way of doing things. What do you think and how can I go about changing this dynamic?

As long as your executive director wants to function as the sole link to your board, so be it. Even though it might seem cumbersome at times, it must remain the executive director's call. For you to operate otherwise could easily result in considerable confusion, if not your outright dismissal.

But there are times when your director's behavior wouldn't be appropriate, such as when he or she has assigned you to be the liaison for a particular committee, commission, or task force of the board or when a staff person has been invited by

4.1   the director to perform any particular function with the board.

As for changing this dynamic, I suggest you not even try. Just be very clear with your executive director in terms of what needs to be communicated to your board and why. In addition, I hope you can openly share your feelings about the procedure (i.e., feelings of being restricted, blocked or bound-in). My guess is that this kind of forthright dialogue will open up and strengthen communication between the two of you and result in an increasingly effective relationship.

4.2   ## ■ *Autocratic Executive Director*

I'm between a rock and a hard place. I care deeply about our organization, yet I see it coming apart. The problem is, our new executive director is an autocrat - he does everything he can not to share power with the board. He takes on their responsibilities, he politely ignores their suggestions, and he's disingenuous to the nth degree. I can see even our most devoted board members losing interest. Is there anything I can do? I've worked with the chair of the executive committee before, but is it wise to interpose myself here?

I have great respect and admiration for your concern regarding the well-being of your organization. But please, do *not* interpose yourself between the executive director and the chair of the executive committee. If you do, you'll be severely compromised and possibly get blind-sided.

Instead, I suggest you have a face-to-face session with your executive director during which time you share some of your observations and feelings. Your basic assumption in this conversation should be that the executive director wants to **4.2** do an effective job in providing top staff leadership for the organization.

Your job, as evidenced by this meeting, is to help him do what he already wants to do by sharing with him data (observations, insights, and feelings) which he does not have and which you hope will be helpful.

Be prepared to get some defensive reactions. Don't be surprised by this, but do try to listen and understand. Perhaps you can be helpful to him and to the organization. I hope so. If not, you have acted responsibly and given it your best shot. At that time you may want to consider interposing yourself, but recognize the risk and do this only as a last resort.

■ *Meddling Board*   **4.3**

My board fancies itself an organizational watchdog ("bulldog" is what I'd call them). I respect that. They are, after all, ultimately responsible for the organization. The problem is, they delegate very little to me (the director). Nearly everything I or my staff does requires board approval and anything I bring before them becomes a trial. Two questions: how can I free myself from this trap, and how can I keep the board a little at bay?

It sounds like your board is certainly fulfilling its monitoring function - in fact, it's probably going too far and making you dependent on them. What you have is a dysfunctional situation that will lead to ever-increasing tension and anxiety among both board and staff members. In short, it won't work and must be stopped.

To free yourself from this trap, I suggest you first be sure

4.3 where the dysfunction is coming from. You say the *board* fancies itself a watchdog. My experience is that, rather than the entire board, this is usually one or two - and not more than three - members. Who are these persons?

After determining where the dysfunction lies, I suggest you sit down with your chief volunteer officer (CVO) and share exactly what you're experiencing - both the source(s) and the consequences of the dysfunction. Do this even if your CVO is part of the problem.

From this discussion, it's imperative you and your CVO agree on the role and major functions of the board and staff - namely, that policy, funding, monitoring, and approval responsibilities are functions of the board, while administrative, managerial, and program responsibilities are the province of the staff.

Once you and the CVO have adequately clarified and agreed on these matters, the CVO must intervene, as necessary, with either individual board members or with the board as a whole to rectify the situation.

Regarding your second question, I don't think you should even try to hold your board at bay. Rather, you need to direct their energies toward carrying out their functions. In addition, they must allow you to carry out your staff functions.

Finally, I suggest you practice a little prevention in the future by placing increased emphasis on an annual board orientation in which board/staff roles, functions, and relationships are worked through, clarified, and agreed upon.

■ *Changing a Staff-Driven Organization*

I was just hired to take over the reins of this organization. The problem is my predecessor called all the shots with the board. Whatever she said, went. No questions invited, no questions asked. I don't want an organization that's so staff-driven. Will you give me a handful of steps I can take immediately to starting changing the dynamic here?

To my knowledge, there's no quick fix for this one. It's going to take some time so don't get discouraged if progress seems slow. Here are some steps you can start on now:

Step 1:

Share your feelings and observations with your board chair. Be open and forthright, but don't in any way denigrate your predecessor. Get the support of your chair to discuss these feelings with the board and ask him or her to appoint a board development committee.

Step 2:

Make your presentation to the board at the next meeting in essentially the same way as you talked with the board chair. The chair should be prepared to appoint a board development committee and the new committee chair should announce the time and date of the first meeting.

Step 3:

Meet with the board development committee and help them to finalize their commission and to understand the difference between a board development committee and a nominating committee. Typically, a nominating committee annually recommends a slate of board members and, sometimes, officers.

4.4

A board development committee also does this, but, in addition, is responsible for overall development of the board (i.e., cultivation and recruitment of new members, annual assessment of members, orientation and training, evaluation, and recognition).

Step 4:

With your help, the chair of the board development committee administers the questionnaire to the board at its next meeting. It will be helpful if the questionnaire can be scored, tabulated, reported, and discussed at this board meeting. The desired outcome is the board's agreement on three to five board development priorities for the coming year.

Step 5:

Work with the board development committee in developing action plans to achieve each of these priorities. Place the action plans themselves in priority order and begin implementation. Based on your question, I'm betting that one of your board development priorities will be a board orientation session focusing on the role and functions of the board and its members and relationships with staff. If that's the case, a well-done board orientation should give you a big boost forward.

The above five steps will get you started, but remember board development is a continuous process so "keep on keeping on."

■ *Attracted to a Board Member* 4.5

I'm very attracted to one of our new board members (and she to me, I think). I'm afraid it'll cause complications. How can I (the director) best separate this rapidly advancing personal relationship from the business of my organization? Help! before it becomes a fatal distraction.

You didn't mention one very important piece of information - is either of you married? If so, the issue is much more serious and crucial for your organization.

If either of you is married, the two of you must decide which is more important - your personal relationship or your respective positions with the organization. Under these circumstances, it's not fair to you, your significant other, or your organization, to stay in your position. Indeed, I think it *will* become a fatal distraction. So, resign or desist.

On the other hand, if you're both single, just be sure you're not partying too much on "company" time. Further, if your relationship continues to deepen, you should probably inform your board chair before too long.

■ *Staff Misconceptions about Boards* 4.6

What would you say are the two or three most common misconceptions nonprofit staff hold about boards?

The first misconception I hear all too frequently is: "Board members are simply a 'pain' - they take a lot of 'care and feeding' and contribute very little."

4.6

A second one voiced almost as often is, "Board members don't really care about the agency. They're in this solely for status and self-aggrandizement."

Unfortunately, there's a modicum of truth in each of these misconceptions. In the main, however, board members make unique contributions that staff should be aware of and appreciate. As I see it, board members bring the following to the agency:

❑ Knowledge and understanding of the needs and potential of the community.

❑ Special abilities, skills, and insights which the agency could never purchase.

❑ Influence for attracting financial, human, and public resources.

❑ Ability to commend the agency to the community and to particular segments of the community.

❑ Objectivity and the capacity for critical review.

❑ Credibility and community confidence in the agency and its work.

The above are only illustrative. Why don't you and your staff see what you can develop?

4.7

■ *Should Board Meetings Be Open to Staff?*

Do you believe board meetings should be open to all staff and not just to the executive director? If not, why not? If yes, please describe the benefits as you see them.

The executive director, as head of the staff, needs to make the call regarding staff attendance at board meetings. In part it's a function of size. Organizations with small staffs (about three full-time persons) typically have everyone attending because they provide staff support to board committees and are needed as resources to the total board. On the other hand, when large staffs attend board meetings they tend to dominate through sheer numbers.

4.7

In general, I think the executive director should have the staff resources present that are needed to ensure effective board functioning. In addition, it's helpful for the executive director periodically to invite different staff to attend board meetings even when they don't have a role in the meeting. This practice can help staff become familiar with the way the board operates and it also gives the board a chance to meet staff members.

Care should be continuously exerted, however, to make certain staff do not dominate board meetings by either participation or attendance. Besides, somebody needs to keep the store open.

■ *Three Common Problems in Dealing with Boards*

4.8

I've just been hired to head a good-sized cultural organization. While I have administrative experience, being an executive director will be a new experience. I'm wondering if you can help prepare me for the job by citing the three most common problems directors have when working with their boards?

My nomination for the three most common problems are undoubtedly influenced by the fact that you're new to the

4.8 position. Nevertheless, they are:

❑ *Giving inadequate attention to the relationship with the board chair.*

I think you need to meet with your board chair at least weekly in the beginning. It takes time and investment to develop a relationship. Work at creating trust through mutual candor and openness. There will be many issues and concerns on which to assist each other. But don't forget your joint responsibilities: agenda building, committee structure and appointments, strategic planning, problem solving, and board development.

❑ *Inadequate board orientation and consequent lack of clarity on the role, functions, and relationships of the board.*

I continue to find that many problems in working with boards could be averted through a comprehensive and interactive board orientation.

❑ *Succumbing to the temptation to dominate the board by information control.*

Many executive directors either consciously or unconsciously attempt to dominate the board by controlling the information flow - letting the board know only what they want them to know. The result: an uninformed board that is vulnerable to being "blind-sided."

■ *Bogged Down in Operating Details*

I've got the opposite problem from some of my colleagues. My board is almost too involved in our organization. They're always second-guessing me (the director) and my fund raising staff. How can I gracefully pry them from my back?

Your problem may be unusual but it's a serious one and can be detrimental. My hunch is that your trustees aren't *too* involved but rather involved in the wrong things, namely, operations and management functions.

One of the major failures of nonprofit boards is getting bogged down in operating detail instead of governing. Sometimes intelligent individuals, and even astute business people, toss aside the principles of good management and common sense and plunge headlong into operating minutiae when they become nonprofit board members. The result? Policy functions, a major responsibility of your board, go unfilled.

One way to get your board out of day-to-day operations is to refocus their efforts on those functions that are under their purview, such as planning, formulating, and adopting policy.

Using your next board meeting, or some other forum of your choosing, get your board cracking on questions such as: Where are we going in the future? What is our strategy for getting there? What is our long-range financial development strategy? How will the board monitor progress and provide support for achieving our goals and objectives? Boards that focus on these kinds of questions don't have time to interfere in operations.

But I can't let this critical matter pass without noting the

4.9 importance and relevance of another factor, namely, board orientation. Every board should have an annual orientation during which board and staff roles are clarified, as are functions and relationships (i.e., who does what?), and the crucial difference between governance and operations. Even when these matters are made clear at the outset, however, they will need to be reinforced periodically by your board chair.

4.10 ## ■ *Executive Director on the Board Too?*

Is it advisable, in your opinion, for an organization's chief executive officer to hold a seat on the board?

I firmly believe that the CEO should *not* hold a seat on the board, though he or she should attend all board meetings and be an integral part of all board activities.

There are some very practical reasons for this. First, some funders won't contribute to an organization that has anyone on the board who benefits financially.

Second, there are times when the CEO can be much more effective - and objective - if he or she doesn't have to take a position and defend it to the board.

Third, having the CEO on the board further confuses the difference between governance and management functions.

I have two client organizations whose CEOs actually started the organizations and nourished them through early hardships. Because of their intense proprietary interests, both CEOs seated themselves on the board and found it very difficult to resign in order to perform the CEO functions.

But in both cases, once the CEOs did resign their seats,

the boards increasingly took responsibility and developed beautifully in partnership with the CEOs.

It's tough for some CEOs who have traditionally held board seats to give them up. Some perceive this as a base of power. But my experience is that when a CEO does resign from the board and calls upon the board to perform its governance functions in collaboration with staff, it represents a sharing of power which significantly moves the organization forward.

4.10

■ *Mutual Appreciation of Board & Staff Roles*

4.11

Please describe for me the best way to encourage volunteers and staff to understand and appreciate each other's role. Is this best done formally, as in a board meeting? Or can it be accomplished casually? I sense some smoldering resentments and misunderstandings and feel if we enhance communication more productivity will result. What's your thinking?

I'm all for enhancing communication, but it's not a panacea, and certainly not in a situation where knowledge and understanding are apparently deficient.

The subject of board and staff roles, functions, and relationships needs to be an integral part of an organization's board orientation program. It doesn't sound like you've had such a program.

It also seems you have a near-emergency on your hands so I suggest you act immediately by conducting a special training session, formal not casual, that focuses on board and staff roles.

4.11   This session will take approximately one hour and can be conducted in conjunction with a regular board meeting or as a special training session. The necessary components of such a session are the following:

❑ Some kind of framework for board members to use in understanding and sorting out responsibilities. One that I like and have found helpful and practical is an adaptation of Arthur Swift's original conceptualization:

Function	Primary Responsibility
Policy & planning formulation	board & staff
Policy & planning determination	board
Policy & planning implementation	staff
Policy & planning monitoring	board & staff

❑ "Who Does What" - an instrument showing a variety of typical agency activities, on which attendees are asked to indicate who holds primary responsibility for each activity - board, staff, or joint. Discussion and clarification follows.

❑ Clear identification of the unique contributions that both board members and staff bring to the agency and to their roles.

❑ Dysfunctions that can and do occur in board and staff relationships.

❑ An outline of the fundamental principles to consider when trying to establish strong and productive board and staff relationships.

You can find resources for these components in several books on board functioning.

■ *Tension Between Board Chairperson and CEO*

What do you do when your board chair obviously dislikes you and shows it in meetings? I've been the CEO of this organization for the past seven years and have gotten along fine with everyone but this individual who assumed the chairperson's post earlier this year. I love this place too much simply to walk away.

I suggest you first engage in a bit of introspection to see if you can understand what's behind this person's dislike of you. Be honest with yourself and try to see the situation from your chairperson's point of view. You might, as a result, decide to make some behavioral changes.

If not, I suggest you schedule a private session with your chairperson in a setting protected from telephone interference and other disturbances.

Basically, this should be a non-directive interview in which you attempt to understand any dysfunctions existing in your relationship. Begin your meeting with a very broad statement like, "Since we have to work so closely as board chair and CEO, I thought it would be a good idea to talk about our relationship. I'd be interested in your thoughts and feelings." Then listen actively for meaning.

Strive for objectivity and understanding during the session and demonstrate your respect for the board chair as a person. This is an opportunity to identify your own prejudices, biases, and blind spots, if any, that may be adversely affecting your relationship. Again, this may lead to new understanding on your part and result in some behavioral changes.

If this doesn't work, have another private session with the

4.12 board chair in which you share very explicitly how you feel as a result of his or her actions, particularly those in board meetings. In addition, discuss the behavioral changes you've made in an attempt to improve the situation.

You might also stress how the two of you need to work together on improving your relationship in the interest of giving more effective leadership to your organization. At a minimum you should agree that individual criticism and critical feedback will be given privately and not in the presence of the board.

If none of these suggestions works, you may have to ride out his or her term in office with as little disruption to the organization as possible. Also, keep in mind that, though desirable, persons working together do not have to like each other as individuals to effectively lead an organization.

4.13
■ *CEO Desires Accountability*

I'm probably cutting my nose to spite my face but as the executive director I don't feel the board holds me accountable enough. Understand, I don't want to be put on a leash, but I do want the board to be more involved and to hold me up to standards that they themselves set. I guess what I'm saying is that I want my performance measured. Am I crazy?

Not by a long shot. In fact, research indicates that the vast majority of CEO's in nonprofits want to be accountable and want to know how they are doing. Unfortunately, research also shows that most nonprofit boards don't provide systematic performance appraisals for CEO's. At best, most offer highly informal feedback on a sporadic basis. This represents a substantial loss to both the CEO's and the organizations involved.   **4.13**

My experience is that CEO performance appraisal is awkward for most boards and many simply don't know how to do it in an objective and helpful manner. Fortunately, some excellent resources are available. As a start, you might check with your own support structure (national associations, professional societies). Also browse through some books on the subject.

Regardless of the performance appraisal method used, care should be taken to ensure that:

❑ It is participative, that is, the CEO contributes by providing performance summaries and appropriate analysis.

❑ It involves two-way communication between the board (or its appointed subgroup) and the CEO.

❑ It is based on performance criteria and not personality traits.

❑ It focuses on job relevant behavior, not unrelated factors.

❑ It is based *primarily* on the organization's performance in achieving its major objectives and on the CEO's managerial effectiveness in specific performance areas.

WORKINGS OF THE BOARD

5

WORKINGS
OF THE BOARD

■ *Common Problems that Beset Boards*

In your opinion, what are the three most common problems that beset boards and how can each of these problems be addressed?

Your question presents a real challenge but I'll take a shot. From my own experience, my nomination for the three most common problems are:

❑ *The wrong criteria are used in selecting people to serve.*

Board members should not be selected simply because they are nice, friendly people. Neither should they be chosen purely on the basis of personal friendships. Board members should be recruited because they have the attributes, abilities, and skills necessary to move the organization forward.

❑ *Inability or reluctance of board members to use their talents while serving on the board.*

The reasons for this are many: members haven't been

5.1 given responsibility; the responsibility they have been given is ill-defined; board meetings are dull, unproductive, and virtual turnoffs; the board chair and chief executive (or others) have already decided on major policies and plans; orientation has been inadequate.

❑ *Large omissions, or put another way, boards leave undone those things which they should do.*

The job of the board is to govern - to formulate policies and plans, to employ, support and evaluate the CEO; to ensure adequate resources are available; and to monitor progress and provide sanction (approval) in the community. All too many boards lose sight of these critical tasks and become involved in day-to-day operations, which is the province of staff.

How might these problems be addressed? Some solutions are clear simply from identifying the problem. For example, if the problem is "wrong selection criteria" as described above, a simplified solution might be, "Specify the selection criteria needed to move the organization forward."

Each reader can and should generate his or her own solutions to these problems. Some will be evident and relatively simple. Others will be much more involved.

5.2 ■ *Board Development Committee*

Do you think it's a good idea to supplement our board development committee with an advisory committee? If so, what should be the selection criteria?

I assume by "board development committee" you mean a group that is responsible for building and continuously developing your organization's board of directors.

5.2

This is quite different from a "development committee of the board," which is a group responsible, with the CEO, for providing leadership in generating the financial resources you need to achieve your long-range goals and short-term objectives.

If we are talking about the former (board development committee), then I don't think you need to supplement this group with an advisory committee. If you need additional resources on your board development committee (including non-board members), then simply go out and recruit them.

While I understand that the last thing most nonprofits need is another committee, I'm glad to hear you have a board development committee. Board development is so crucial it merits the detailed oversight and effort of a committee.

In fact, I recommend the traditional nominating committee be replaced by a board development committee whose functions go far beyond those of a typical nominating committee.

To me, board development is an ongoing process of building and developing a board that will preserve and enhance the character, growth, and influence of the agency and maximize its contribution in the lives of the people and in the community it serves.

Among the key components a board development committee should address are:
- ❑ Assessment of board members
- ❑ Identification of needed board members
- ❑ Rotation
- ❑ Retention
- ❑ Cultivation
- ❑ Recruitment

5.2

❑ Organization and effective functioning
❑ Orientation
❑ Use of members' resources
❑ Training and education
❑ Evaluation
❑ Recognition

Board development is a big job, one that merits the attention of the organization's top leadership and a fully functioning board development committee. But I don't think a board development committee needs an advisory committee. Just do it!

5.3

■ *Effective Use of Committees*

Our committee structure is very weak, one reason being that our board president likes to have everything discussed at board meetings. It's her version of the Sunshine Law. The result of her good intention, however, is that almost every policy decision comes before the full board for debate. And you can imagine how much time this leaves for other matters. How can I, the executive director, get her to use committees more effectively?

Admittedly, this is a difficult issue. You certainly want your board to be well-informed and not function as a rubber stamp. On the other hand, the board cannot always do the detailed analysis and engage in active debate about all recommendations or it will get bogged down and diverted from its central responsibility of determining policy.

In your case it may be that committees are not functioning adequately, either because they don't know what's expected of them or they're convinced the board itself will redo their work by acting as a committee of the whole. In either case, it can become a Catch 22.

I suggest you and the board president meet with committee chairs and provide them with an outline for making committee recommendations (i.e., problem statement, analysis, alternative solutions, recommendations).

The outline might also include other matters, as appropriate, such as estimated costs, environmental impact, relationship to your strategic plan, and the like. It would also be a good idea to have the committees' recommendations submitted in writing and mailed to all board members for their study and review prior to the board meeting.

My guess is that using such a procedure will make clear to your board president and to board members themselves that starting from square one on each committee recommendation is not only dysfunctional, it is a waste of the board's time.

If this doesn't work, it may be that your board president simply thinks that committees are an ineffective mechanism for formulating policy. Perhaps she believes committees are a waste of time or maybe she agrees with the wag who said, "A committee is a collection of individuals who separately do nothing and together decide that nothing can be done." If so, you may need to review with your board president the advantages of committees.

You probably have you own list of advantages and I encourage you to use it with your president. As I see it, among the most important benefits of committees are that they:

❑ Relieve board meetings of many routine matters;

❑ Maximize the opportunities for involving board members and using their resources through detailed work on worthy tasks;

❑ Offer the board the chance to use special resources of

5.3   agency members or supporters that may not be on the board itself;

❏ Improve the quality of policy formulation and problem-solving through small group work that allows careful, and detailed consideration of data, issues, and alternatives; and,

❏ Ensure that all essential factors in carrying out the agency's work are given adequate consideration.

5.4   ## ■ *Reimbursement Abuse*

I've got a delicate problem that's gotten out of hand. This agency has a tradition of reimbursing its board members for expenses incurred while attending meetings (mileage, lodging, food, even child care). The problem is, every single one of our members, including my chairperson, has grown accustomed to abusing this tradition. It's like a contagion now. They stay at the best hotels, eat at the best restaurants, some have the gall to fly first class. I'm the frugal CEO who gets the shocking reimbursement vouchers and am at a loss at how to stop this across-the-board abuse.

Let's hear it for frugality! I'm with you and I fully support your desire to stop the insanity!

If you have a policy or specific guidelines for reimbursement of expenses, enforce the policy. Begin with a memo from the board chair to all board members prior to the next meeting. This will obviously require considerable discussion between you and the chair since the chair is one of the offenders.

It may be that you have a reimbursement policy but it does not contain specific guidelines (i.e., no amount per mile for reimbursement, no dollar-cap for meals and lodging, no specification of tourist class airfare). If this is the case, then **5.4** your human resource committee needs to go to work on providing specific reimbursement guidelines for both board and staff.

Of course, if you don't have any reimbursement policy and guidelines, then the committee needs to get cracking on developing them. In either case, you can be helpful by retrieving reimbursement specifics from other similar organizations.

The fact that your agency has a widespread tradition of reimbursement extravagance may present a considerable obstacle to effecting meaningful change. But here are some points that might be useful in motivating your board and the human resource committee to act:

❑ The practices of other organizations, as previously noted.

❑ The need for a policy that includes reimbursement guidelines for all the organization's human resources - board and staff.

❑ Budget constraints and the critical need to use scarce funds for programs and services.

❑ The fact that board and staff can exceed the expense guidelines as they desire (i.e. they can fly first class if they wish), but they will be reimbursed only in accord with the guidelines.

You can also remind them of the scandal surrounding the United Way of America's former national executive in his alleged abuse of expense reimbursements. Don't let this happen to your board members or staff.

Finally, let me say that it is reasonable and, in many cases, necessary for large national and regional agencies to provide meeting expense reimbursement for board members. Not to

5.4 do this will limit board membership only to those who can afford to incur considerable travel expenses.

However, I do suggest placing a statement at the bottom of your reimbursement vouchers - something like, "Less amount of meeting expenses incurred which I wish to contribute to the agency."This provides another opportunity for board members to contribute to the agency at their discretion and within their means.

5.5 ■ *Ensuring Follow-Through After Meetings*

At most of our board meetings, assignments are made, accepted and duly recorded. However, by the time the next meeting rolls around, it's as if everyone has forgotten (or to be more precise, ignored) what they were supposed to do. The result? A lot of redundancy and spinning wheels. What in your opinion is the best tactic to follow between meetings to ensure that everyone follows through?

Here are some tactics your board chair can use:

❑ Indicating at the time of agreement or appointment when a report to the total board will be called for.

❑ Calling the member or members between meetings to inquire about progress.

❑ Reminding the responsible persons of the forthcoming reporting meeting.

❑ Offering help, support, and encouragement to those who have accepted assignments.

These suggestions, of course, can be accomplished by sending a letter, but a personal call is much more effective.

In larger organizations where many volunteer assignments have a corollary staff-support assignment, it's sometimes helpful and proper for the staff person to call the volunteer with such inquiries as: "Is there anything I can do now to get us started in this assignment?" or "When can we get together to begin thinking about our assignment?" or "What material or information do you think you might need that I can help pull together?"

5.5

Such gentle nudges and indications of support will usually get things rolling but, if not, the board chair might have to speak at the next board meeting about the inefficiency of redundancy and wheel-spinning and the importance of teamwork, interdependence and what I call "colleague accountability" among board members.

■ *How Many Committees?*

5.6

In terms of board committees, which theory do you subscribe to and why: the more the merrier or the fewer the better?

I come down on the side of having relatively few standing committees. Most nonprofits have far too many and they are "repeaters" - reappearing every year whether or not they're needed.

This isn't necessary and it may not be possible to function effectively with more than four to six standing committees. Having more runs the risk of spreading the board and staff resources too thin (and they may even end up stumbling over one another).

Some argue that organizations should have as many committees as possible - the more the merrier - in order to

5.6 involve people, deepen their commitment, and make them feel a part. There are, however, effective ways of involving people other than locking them into standing committees.

I have in mind ad hoc groups, temporary teams, task forces, and project teams - groups formed, usually for a short or prescribed time, to accomplish specific tasks. I'm a great proponent of these ad hoc groups and "temporary systems."

Let me be clear - I'm not against committees. Committees are important. They represent a major method of organizing the work of boards and a way of getting the board's job done. Yeah, I know, you probably have your favorite one-liner that degrades committees. One of my favorites is: "A committee is an assemblage of the unwilling, deciding the unnecessary, at the request of the uncaring."

But despite all the humor and wise remarks, committees are important and we need them - just not too many of them.

5.7 ■ *Ensuring Successful Meetings*

Please give me a prescription for successful board meetings. That is, what are six or seven things I can do to help ensure our meetings are productive and harmonious?

Here are seven things you can, and should, do beforehand to help make your board meetings more productive.

❏ Consider the setting. It must be attractive, comfortable, and conducive to productive work. Accessibility, convenient parking and, if applicable, good quality food service also help.

❏ Arrange seating to elicit participation. A large round table encourages involvement as does "hollow square"

seating where members face the center. Avoid the traditional **5.7**
"lecture" or "classroom" arrangement.

❑ Always put in the agenda something of true significance - an important item that needs the board's consideration. If you don't have at least one such item on the docket, cancel the meeting.

❑ Send the agenda, including all printed reports and reference materials, at least one week in advance for review and study.

❑ Occasionally, hold meetings in special settings - a branch building, program center, or an affiliate's facility.

❑ Give "planned attention" to maximizing the involvement of all board members in discussion, review, and decision-making activities.

❑ Accompany your agenda mailing with an "RSVP" postcard and make a reminder call to each member either on the day before or the day of the meeting.

There are of course other things you can do to help promote productive and harmonious meetings, but these should get you off to a good start.

■ *The Ideal Executive Committee*   5.8

Describe for me the ideal executive committee and how it functions.

To me an executive committee, typically composed of the board's officers and possibly the chairs of some committees, is ideally a clearing, coordinating and/or review group. Its major function is to act, but only as necessary, between meetings of the full board. It can of course be assigned additional functions by the board, such as evaluating the

5.8 | CEO's performance.

In my judgment, which may strike you as extreme or radical, there are some drawbacks or even dangers to having an executive committee. In all too many cases, executive committees act in place of boards and risk making the board, in perception if not in fact, a useless appendage that functions only as a rubber stamp. When this happens, it effectively limits the ownership base of the organization and can be very detrimental.

It may be necessary or important for your organization to have an executive committee that can serve on an interim basis. But don't take it as an absolute - give it serious consideration and question whether you really need it.

5.9 | ## ■ *Committee Crazy?*

I'm afraid, in our desire to be inclusive, that we've become committee crazy. In your opinion, what are the core committees we need and how do we go about disbanding some of our non-essential ones?

I share your concern regarding "committee craziness." It seems to me that most nonprofits have far too many standing committees and retain some committees each year even when they're not needed. I don't think it's necessary and, depending on the size and nature of your organization, it may not be possible to function effectively with more than four to six standing committees.

Be careful not to spread board and staff resources so thin that "attending committee meetings" become the primary component of your job description.

You should know, however, that not all experts agree **5.9** with me. One of my colleagues for whom I have the highest regard feels that the more committees you have, the better. I respectfully disagree.

I think most agencies need the following standing committees:

1) Program committee

2) Budget and finance committee

3) Strategy development committee (dealing primarily with long-term financial development strategy.

4) Property management committee (if the agency holds property to any large extent)

5) Board development committee (concerned with developing a productive board).

There are, of course, many other possibilities, most of which can be appointed as ad hoc committees. These might include personnel/employee relations, public relations & marketing, capital development, and corporate planning.

As for disbanding committees, I suggest your board chair simply not reappoint them. Appoint productive members to other committees, ad hoc groups, or provide specific assignments.

5.10 ## ■ *Should Nonprofits Be Run Like Businesses?*

What is fast becoming an old saw is the statement that nonprofits should operate more like businesses. I've always been ambivalent about this, maybe because I've never seen a good exposition of the ways a nonprofit should operate like a business (and the ways it shouldn't). Can you supply it, please?

In general, I don't think nonprofits should be run like businesses - at least not like some businesses I'm familiar with. This isn't to say business techniques and approaches can't be effectively used by nonprofits. Obviously they can and should be.

Consider for a moment where many nonprofits would be without techniques such as cost analysis, budgeting, auditing, and quality management to name a few. In addition, there are many people-oriented techniques such as team development, organizational interfacing, and a multitude of empowering processes drawn from the business sector.

In my opinion, however, these are not so much techniques of business as they are techniques of management. The practice of good management is proper to the success of any organized pursuit and not the exclusive province of business.

Suffice it to say that all nonprofit organizations should be effectively managed to achieve their mission in the lives of people and in the community they serve. It is my hope that these organizations will use the learning and techniques from all sectors - business, government, and nonprofits - and not be diverted from their central task by so-called "old saws."

■ *Lurching From Crisis to Crisis* 5.11

My organization lurches from crisis to crisis, emergency to emergency. I plead with the board to plan, to hold a retreat, to attend a management seminar, anything! But the responses I get are: Plan! There's no time to plan; or, If we developed a plan, nobody would follow it anyway; or, We don't even know if we can meet payroll this month, let alone plan. I believe in what our organization does, but I can't bear this state of affairs much longer.

The resistance you face is common. So many people have experienced planning as taking an inordinate amount of time and producing few, if any, tangible results. Believe me, I've heard the same comments and many more. In fact, I thought I'd heard every resistance possible until recently a board member in one of my client organizations espoused a new one: "We were making money in my business until we starting writing everything down."

I suggest having a heart-to-heart discussion with your board chair and one other board member who you think would be a prime prospect for your Planning Committee (probably the CEO or a top officer of a major corporation). Share your feelings with them, much as you have done here. Clearly identify the problems that your organization is facing that are directly attributable to the lack of planning or to the inadequacy of planning in the past.

You will, I bet, still encounter resistance from other board members. If so, I suggest you ask them to evaluate individually the effect that planning could have on your organization.

Several good instruments are available to do this but, as you might expect, I prefer my own (as set forth in my book,

5.11 *Managing for Impact in Nonprofit Organizations).*

In a single board meeting, you can conduct this exercise, tabulate results, and discuss how the group can strengthen its planning processes. I've used this approach with several boards and it hasn't failed yet to clarify the need for planning and to generate support for moving ahead.

One caution - before launching the evaluation, be sure you have a plan for going forward. For example, you need to be clear on the whole planning process itself; how you intend to get genuine involvement from all members without being unduly demanding of their time; and how you expect to implement and monitor the process to get real results.

Do this well and you'll be pleasantly surprised at the support you generate, both for your own leadership and for real planning in your organization.

5.12

■ *Handling Out-of-Control Meetings*

My board chair is very weak when it comes to managing meetings and people. As a result, our meetings tend to get out of hand, sometimes with people even shouting at one another. While they make for good theatre, these combustible meetings tend to be harmful to our organization. How can I bring some sanity back?

At some board meetings I've attended, displays of passion and shouting would be a breath of fresh air. But it's a problem for you so here are some suggestions.

First, you and the board chair should convene a meeting of the officers to acknowledge jointly the problem and to brainstorm some possible solutions. Don't leave this meeting

without agreeing on what is to be done, who's going to do it, | **5.12**
and when it will take place. If this doesn't result in noticeable
improvement, move on to the following approach.

Second, at the next meeting of the board, the chair should
spend a few minutes "framing" the problem (i.e., describing
it with some examples). The board should then be placed in
small groups and asked to develop "Behavioral guidelines for
all members of the board for making meetings more
productive."

Let these small groups work for about 15 minutes and
then report out. Either you or the chair should post the
guidelines, as this will give you the opportunity to clarify each
one as reports are made. The chair then states his or her
expectation that all board members will both abide by the
guidelines and monitor other members and publicly point out
any violations.

Prior to the next meeting, have the guidelines printed for
the chair to review at the beginning of the meeting and call the
board's attention to the importance of adherence by all
members. This should solve your problem but if it doesn't
move to the third approach.

The board chair convenes a meeting of the perpetrators
and the officers and conducts a very candid discussion of the
dysfunctional behaviors which must be stopped at once.

FUND RAISING

....

6

FUND RAISING

■ *To Raise Money or Cut Services?*

Rather than exert more effort raising money, our board would prefer to cut back on the services we offer. Not only would this be a hardship for the people we serve, it's a cop-out for a board with considerable fund raising potential. How can I, the director, keep them from abdicating their responsibility?

Based solely on what you've said, I'm not at all sure your board has abdicated its responsibility. After all, it is their role to make the final determination about your agency's goals and objectives and to acquire and allocate the resources to achieve them.

In my opinion, a board is acting responsibly when it determines what should be accomplished and balances this with its best judgment regarding what is financially feasible.

My experience is that when a board determines that money cannot be generated to achieve particular outcomes, it frequently means the board hasn't been genuinely involved in formulating the goals and objectives.

In such a case, these have been developed by and "belong

119

6.1 to" someone else (i.e. the CEO, the executive committee, the planning committee, or an influential few). The board doesn't "own" the goals and objectives and has little, if any, commitment to them.

If you want to promote genuine ownership of your organization's long-range goals, have a two-day "Future Directions" conference for the board. You'll find detailed guidance for preparing and conducting this kind of conference in numerous books, including my own - *Managing for Impact in Nonprofit Organizations*.

Furthermore, a board's perception of what is possible is directly related to its sense of what is important and vital in the lives of people and in the community.

I suggest you not be so quick to condemn your board for abdicating its responsibility, but that you carefully examine the processes you have used (or not used) for involving them.

I believe if boards are constituted properly, given the necessary data, and provided real opportunities for involvement, they will make decisions that maximize the agency's contributions to people. And they will vigorously uphold those decisions with their time, talent, and treasure.

6.2 ■ *Fund Raising is Not Belittling*

On our board we have a contingent that thinks fund raising is belittling (though of course they'd never come out and say so). Those who do fund raising - and like it no more than this contingent - are beginning to seethe. How do I solve this problem before it sours too many relationships?

It sounds like your organization's rationale for fund

raising hasn't been clearly communicated to the board. If this is correct, then your board chair and chief executive officer need to do this and do it quickly - like at your next board meeting.

Make it clear why you need to raise money (whether it's to provide scholarships for those unable to pay, to subsidize work in low income areas, to send kids to camp, or to provide disaster relief).

Reiterate, clarify, and emphasize that one of the major functions of the board is to develop financial resources. This responsibility cannot be delegated - it must be carried out by all board members.

In carrying out this function, one of the first things board members need to do is to give themselves. Making an annual contribution - within one's means - is not buying a seat on the board, but it is an important act of commitment. Not to give is simply to declare indifference.

Every organization should expect and receive 100 percent financial participation from its board (and its staff too). In addition, board members should participate in annual support efforts by soliciting contributions from others, "opening doors" and making presentations to federated funding agencies, corporations, and foundations.

I recognize that some board members find asking for money distasteful, particularly when it means asking a friend or acquaintance. But as Fisher Howe in *Board Member's Guide to Fund Raising* points out, board members can assist significantly without personally soliciting a contribution, by helping staff in the preparation, cultivating prospects, accompanying others on the solicitation visit, and writing personal notes.

6.2   Ensuring that money is available to achieve your agency's goals is a critical task - one that need not be unpleasant - but one requiring the support and help of all board members.

6.3 ■ *Giving Both Time & Money*

Please give me a good response to the trustee who says, "I give my time, I shouldn't be asked to give money too."

Let me say directly and clearly that *all* trustees are individually responsible for giving fully and enthusiastically of time, money, and expertise as appropriate.

This should be stated during your initial recruiting, restated at the board orientation, and restated yet again if members begin to lapse.

Giving by each individual trustee is directly related to one of the major functions of the board itself, namely, developing the financial resources to achieve goals. Does this mean board members must fund the organization totally from their own means? Not at all. But it does mean they hold the ultimate responsibility for attracting the funding. And, to carry out this responsibility, one of their first actions must be to give themselves.

It is important for board members to provide specific actions that demonstrate their commitment to the organization and its mission. Personal giving - always within one's means - is a visible and absolutely critical way of evidencing commitment and providing an example for others.

■ *Asking Those Not on the Board to Serve*

My development committee needs vitality - desperately. I'd like to bring some non-board members on - some people I know in the community - but I'm not sure it's a good idea. I fear these people will feel like second-class citizens, asked to do the grunt work but not eligible to participate in governing decisions. Is my fear warranted and is it a good idea to ask non-board people to serve?

I don't think your fear is warranted. Quite the contrary, it's a great idea to ask non-board people to serve on committees. New people and new resources can give your committee that desperately needed vitality - assuming they're able, competent, and committed persons.

Moreover, in my experience, I've never known high-caliber people to feel like second-class citizens when asked to serve.

Bringing on non-board people, besides possibly revitalizing your committee, is also a significant way to increase your organization's leadership pool and provide a training and experience arena for prospective board talent.

I especially like the idea because it's two-way: it gives the committee member an opportunity to assess your organization from the inside, to contribute, and to increase commitment, while you and your board committee members can evaluate the person's potential for even greater leadership.

If a non-board member shows enthusiasm and is productive on a committee, you just may have an outstanding board member for the future. It's a win-win situation.

6.5 ■ *Which Campaign Leader?*

If you had to choose one person among the following to lead a fund raising campaign, who would you choose and why? A wealthy person who will give but has limited social skills; a well-liked person in the community with little or no entree to those holding wealth; someone with great clout and a slew of enemies; or a fearless soul with limited experience raising money.

I'd choose the wealthy person who will give but has limited social skills, if he or she agrees to the required time commitment. My rationale is a simple one: this individual can and apparently will make a substantial contribution, thus setting the pace for others. Also, people of means often have easier access to, and influence on, other persons of wealth.

I would also find a place in the campaign for the others, except the one with a slew of enemies. You certainly don't need nor want to inherit, even by association, an army of enemies. The other two people can be helpful both now and in the future - particularly the "fearless soul." You can provide the training and experience and he or she can provide the assertiveness and the "fire."

6.6 ■ *Can't Give, Can't Ask?*

Please present your most persuasive counter-argument for a board member who protests: "I can't give much myself, so I can't ask."

Although I'll probably sound like Pollyanna, the amount one gives is relatively unimportant. But the act of giving -

within one's means - is of vital consequence.   **6.6**

It is an act of commitment to the organization's mission, goals, programs, and services. It is an act of caring for people and for the quality of life in the community.

Giving in this way, as a genuine expression of commitment and caring, is the ultimate qualification for soliciting gifts from others.

It can be, and should be, made known to those who are being solicited that all board members have given.

■ *Be Candid About the*   **6.7**
Fund Raising Responsibility

My board and executive director, when recruiting a new trustee, always hedge when it comes to that person's role with respect to fund raising. They can't bring themselves to be direct and candid and to say that contributing money and soliciting others is part and parcel of the board member's job. How can I get them to level with promising candidates or is there some end run that I, as development director, should take?

No end runs, please! I suggest you first go directly to your executive director and get his or her full support for "giving and getting funds" as an integral part of a board member's job. Regardless of your organization's income streams (United Way, grants, membership dues, program fees, earned income), surely your executive director recognizes the absolute necessity of contributions income for providing what one of my colleagues calls "the extra margin."

This margin is critical - it allows your organization to move from fair to good, from good to excellent, and from excellent to outstanding.

6.7   If your executive director doesn't understand and fully support this notion and, if you cannot make a dent in his or her armor, I suggest you update your resume and start looking for an organization whose leadership wants it to contribute maximally in its service to people and to the community.

But, assuming you get through to your executive director, then the two of you need to have a "heart to heart" conversation with the board chair and the chair of the nominating committee.

Once you have the full understanding and support of these leaders, be sure this key board responsibility of giving and soliciting funds from others is included in all board documentation and processes - board members' job descriptions, orientation materials on role, functions, and responsibilities of board members, and in all recruiting material and training designs for recruitment teams.

6.8   ## ■ *Staff Can't Raise the Money Alone*

One of our longest serving board members continually says things like, "We just need to find a fat cat to fund this." He also implies what we (meaning me, the development professional) should be able to get most of our needed funding - from foundations. How can I educate him and others about fund raising today?

I suggest saying to him that if he knows of a fat cat, "Go after him and let me know what I can do to be supportive." It's a long shot, but maybe he can come up with something.

It's more likely this won't happen, however. Then you will have to explain to him that the odds of finding a fat cat are long and that what your organization needs are many well-heeled people who believe deeply in what you're about and want to help you do it. **6.8**

I suggest you also let him in on the reality of foundation giving - namely, that foundation grants account for only about five percent of monies given each year to philanthropic causes. Unless your organization has a special entree or a continuing relationship with a foundation, the time and energy can usually be spent more productively on identifying and soliciting individuals, a point you can emphasize to your board member by noting that individuals account for nearly ninety percent of all giving!

As you well know, there's no easy short-cut to fund raising. It's an ongoing and difficult job.

About the Author

Dr. James M. (Bo) Hardy is president of JMH Associates, a management consulting and training firm. He is the author of six books and the editor of four others. Currently he writes a regular column for *Contributions* magazine.

Dr. Hardy received his undergraduate degree in business and psychology from Southwestern University, his master's degree from Harvard Graduate School of Business, and his Ph.D. in organizational development and planning from Union Graduate School.

He is a member of the American Psychological Association, American Management Association, American Society for Training and Development, and the World Future Society.

Although he maintains a heavy schedule, Dr. Hardy is an avid outdoorsman and sports enthusiast. He and his late wife, Bettye, camped in the African bush and the Amazon rain forest; trekked in the Himalayas; camped and rode horseback in New Zealand's Southern Alps; dived the Great Barrier Reef and the Belize Barrier Reef; tracked rhinos by elephant-back in Nepal's Chitwan jungle; and climbed the Great Wall of China and Mt. Fuji in Japan.

Dr. Hardy, the father of three young adults, resides in Pippin Hollow, Erwin, Tennessee.